PRESENTED TO:

_____

Life is fragile—
handle with prayer.

Author Unknown

PRESENTED BY:

_____

Life's Daily Prayer Book for Mothers
©2005 Elm Hill Books
ISBN: 1-404-18520-8

This manuscript written and compiled by Susan Duke and Rebecca
Currington in conjunction with Snapdragon Editorial Group, Inc.

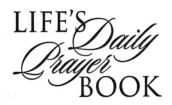

LIFE'S *Daily* *Prayer* BOOK

for Mothers

Prayers to Encourage and Comfort the Soul

Elm Hill Books
An Imprint of J. Countryman®

An old hymn goes: "What a friend we have in Jesus, all our sins and griefs to bear. What a privilege to carry everything to God in prayer." They're wonderful words, aren't they—comforting, strengthening, liberating. And they are words of truth! In the Bible, God invites us to friendship with Him, a friendship that urges us to cast all our cares on Him. Have you ever thought about talking to God as you would to a friend?

Life's Daily Prayer Book for Mothers was designed to guide and inspire you as you reach out to God in friendship and converse with Him concerning the issues, activities, and relationships that impact you as a mother. Think of these written prayers as letters to your best friend—God. Make them your own by adding the names of family and friends and specific needs. And don't forget to record and date your answers. God bless you as you embark on this exciting spiritual adventure.

God always has an open ear and a ready hand, if you have an open and ready heart.

C. H. Spurgeon

Life's Daily Prayer Book for Mothers
Prayers to Encourage and Comfort the Soul

Daily Prayers for . . .

Daily Prayers for Help . . .

Daily Prayers for Guidance . . .

Daily Prayers of Praise for . . .

Prayer is a surge of the heart; it is a simple look turned toward heaven, it is a cry of recognition and of love, embracing both trial and joy.

Thérèse of Lisieux

Daily Prayers . . .

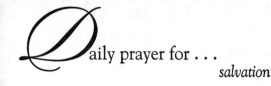
$\mathcal{D}$aily prayer for . . .
salvation

> *"There is salvation in no one else! Under all*
> *heaven there is no other name for men to call*
> *upon to save them."*
>
> Acts 4:12 TLB

Heavenly Father,

I thought being an independent person would make me
the kind of woman and mother I wanted to be—strong
and confident enough to face anything. But, I've grown
weary of frantic searches and temporary solutions. I've
come to the end of my own strength and myself—and
now, Father, I'm desperate for You.

Forgive me for not trusting You as my source and
strength. Forgive me for leaving Your gift of salvation
unopened at the door of my heart. Take full control of
my life right now. From this day forward, I want to be a
woman of faith, a mother of faith—someone who can
teach her children to trust in Your everlasting love.
Thank You for the gift of salvation.

Amen.

So overflowing is his kindness toward us that he took away all our sins
through the blood of his Son, by whom we are saved.
Ephesians 1:7 TLB

MY PERSONAL PRAYER

*Amazing Love! How can it be that
Thou, my God, shouldst die for me?*
Charles Wesley

Dear Father:

_____

_____

_____

_____

_____

_____

Amen

*The Lord is my strength and song,
and He has become my salvation.*
Exodus 15:2 NAS

Thanks be to God for his inexpressible gift!
2 Corinthians 9:15 RSV

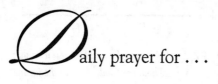 aily prayer for . . .

peace

Jesus said, "Peace I leave with you, My peace I give to you; not as the world gives do I give to you. Let not your heart be troubled, neither let it be afraid."

John 14:27 NIV

Heavenly Father,

This house is full of chaos—fighting, crying, confusion. And I know why. There won't be peace in my home until peace has been established in my heart. Help me as I surrender my troubled heart to You. Quiet all the voices that continue to harass me from within. Fill me up with Your precious Holy Spirit.

Then, Lord, I ask You to pour out Your peace on my children. Replace the conflict with compassion, the despair with hope and the confusion with the orderliness of Your kingdom on earth. I'm depending on You, Lord. And I know that my trust is well placed for You are the God of all peace.

Amen.

Do not be afraid or discouraged, for the Lord is the one who goes before you. He will be with you; he will neither fail you nor forsake you.
Deuteronomy 31:8 NLT

MY PERSONAL PRAYER   *If peace be in the heart, the wildest*
winter storm is full of beauty.
Charles Francis Richardson

Dear Father:

_____

_____

_____

_____

_____

_____

_____

Amen

You will keep him in perfect peace, whose mind is stayed on
You, because he trusts in You.
Isaiah 26:3

Those who know Your name will put their trust in You; for
You, Lord, have not forsaken those who seek You.
Psalm 9:10

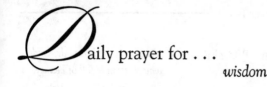

$\mathcal{D}$aily prayer for . . .

wisdom

*Happy is the person who finds wisdom and
gains understanding.*

Proverbs 3:13 NLT

Heavenly Father,

Being a Mom is tough. So tough that I simply can't do it
without Your help. I need Your wisdom and understanding.
Unfortunately I often react without taking the time to
ask You for that help. I know that my children deserve
more. They deserve the very best I can give them, and
that can only come from You.

Lord, I want to become a seeker of Your wisdom.
Someone who takes the time to read Your Word and
wait for Your answers. Someone who is able to put aside
pride and humble herself before You. Someone worthy
of the responsibility of leading her children in the paths
of righteousness.

Amen.

*As the heavens are higher than the earth, so are My ways higher
than your ways, and My thoughts than your thoughts.*

Isaiah 55:9

MY PERSONAL PRAYER

*Wisdom is God-given ability to see
life with rare objectivity and to
handle life with rare stability.*
Charles L. Swindoll

Dear Father:

_____

_____

_____

_____

_____

_____

Amen

*Through wisdom a house is built,
and by understanding it is established.*
Proverbs 24:3

*Wisdom is sweet to your soul. If you find it, you will have a
bright future, and your hopes will not be cut short.*
Proverbs 24:14 NLT

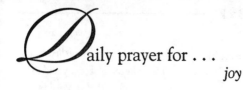

Daily prayer for . . .
joy

The joy of the Lord is your strength.
Nehemiah 8:10

Heavenly Father,

I've been asking myself lately, *Do other people see joy in me? Or have I allowed the cares and demands of life to rob me of my joy as a woman and mother? Do I demonstrate joy to my children; or do they walk on eggshells whenever I'm around?*

Father, I realize that happiness may depend on outward circumstances, but true joy that comes from You is like a constant and ever burning flame in my heart. Forgive me for allowing the everyday cares of life pour water on that flame. Rekindle my heart with the fire of Your presence. Restore me and fill me with the kind of joy that reflects Your steadfast love to my family.

Amen.

You have let me experience the joys of life and the exquisite pleasures of Your own eternal presence.
Psalm 16:11 TLB

MY PERSONAL PRAYER

Where the Savior rules the heart, joy is made complete. Let his love live in you richly, and laughter will come easily.
John William Smith

Dear Father:

_____

_____

_____

_____

_____

_____

Amen

You have endowed him with eternal happiness. You have given him the unquenchable joy of your presence.
Psalm 21:6 TLB

You love him even though you have never seen him. Though you do not see him, you trust him; and even now you are happy with a glorious, inexpressible joy.
1 Peter 1:8 NLT

$\mathcal{D}$aily prayer for . . .
comfort

> *May our Lord Jesus Christ Himself and God our*
> *Father, who has loved us and given us eternal comfort*
> *and good hope by grace, comfort and strengthen your*
> *hearts in every good work and word.*
>
> 2 Thessalonians 2:16-17 NAS

Heavenly Father,

My heart is heavy. I feel helpless and alone. Today I need Your comfort—nothing else and no one else will do.

When my children need comforting, they run to me, and I take them up in my arms and embrace them. Sometimes when they're feeling really bad, we snuggle close and rest. Usually, we don't even need words. Just being together makes us both feel better.

I think today, Lord, is one of those days when I need to feel You very close to me. I need to close my eyes and warm myself in Your presence. Open Your comforting arms to me, I pray. Open them and let me come.

Amen.

> *What a wonderful God we have—he is the Father of our Lord Jesus*
> *Christ, the source of every mercy, and the one who so wonderfully*
> *comforts and strengthens us in our hardships and trials.*
>
> 2 Corinthians 1:3 TLB

MY PERSONAL PRAYER

In Christ the heart of the Father is revealed, and higher comfort there cannot be than to rest in the Father's heart.

Andrew Murray

Dear Father:

_____

_____

_____

_____

_____

_____

Amen

The Lord is near to those who have a broken heart,
and saves such as have a contrite spirit.
Psalm 34:18

Let your unfailing love comfort me,
just as you promised me, your servant.
Psalm 119:76 NLT

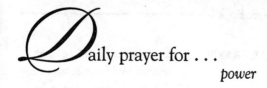

Daily prayer for . . .
power

*God gives power to the weak, and to those
who have no might He increases strength.*
Isaiah 40:29

Heavenly Father,

I'm sure You've noticed that being a mother can be a difficult, stressful job. Sometimes it's sheer heaven and other times, I feel like I'm going to buckle under the weight of it. Raising children is just such an overwhelming responsibility. Each child seems to have his or her own suitcase full of needs that only Mother can fill.

Of course, I'm sure You never intended for me to take on motherhood without Your help. Forgive me, Lord, for trying to do it all on my own. Give me Your power today—power to be all that my children need me to be. The power to be an instrument of Your grace, love, wisdom, joy, peace, and patience. The power to be the mother You created me to be.

Amen.

We praise you, Lord, for all your glorious power.
Psalm 21:13 NLT

MY PERSONAL PRAYER

*God's grace and power are such
none can ever ask too much.*

John Newton

Dear Father:

_____

_____

_____

_____

_____

_____

_____

Amen

*What is the immeasurable greatness of his power in us who
believe, according to the working of his great might.*
Ephesians 1:19 RSV

*We have this treasure in earthen vessels, that the excellence
of the power may be of God and not of us.*
2 Corinthians 4:7

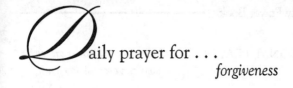

$\mathcal{D}$aily prayer for . . .

forgiveness

You, Lord, are good, and ready to forgive, and
abundant in mercy to all those who call upon You.
Psalm 86:5

Heavenly Father,

I try my best to never do anything that would intentionally cause my children pain. But I admit, I don't always deal with problems in the right way, and I sometimes hurt those I love the most. Please forgive me for my harsh words and actions and also for my angry thoughts and attitudes.

It's just so easy to mess up in this job, Lord. No matter how good my intentions, it seems like there is always something, some little thing, waiting to trip me up— curfews missed, unfinished homework, disobedience, even careless disregard for safety. It's a lot to deal with, but it also keeps me on my knees before You.

So, Lord, I ask You to forgive me where I've failed You by failing my children. Go with me as I begin again.

Amen.

Jesus said, "If you forgive men their trespasses,
your heavenly Father will also forgive you."
Matthew 6:14

MY PERSONAL PRAYER

*Forgiveness is the key to breaking
the cycle of sins passed from one
generation to another.*
Nancy Corbett Cole

Dear Father:

_____

_____

_____

_____

_____

_____

Amen

Feel my pain and see my trouble. Forgive all my sins.
Psalm 25:18 NLT

*Jesus said, "Whenever you stand praying, if you have
anything against anyone, forgive him, that your Father in
heaven may also forgive you your trespasses."*
Mark 11:25

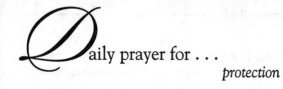

Daily prayer for . . .

protection

*You are my hiding place; you protect
me from trouble.*

Psalm 32:7 NLT

Heavenly Father,

It seems like there are just so many ways to get hurt in this big, old world of ours. I feel like I can't even begin to keep my children safe. Even if I watched them every single moment and never let them leave the house, there are still hazards everywhere. And what about when they are old enough to drive? Well . . . I'll do my best, Lord, but it just isn't possible without Your help.

Once again today, I place my children in Your care. I ask You to send Your angels to watch over them and keep them safe. Literally, that means saving them from their own foolishness and the foolishness of others. I trust You with each precious life.

Amen.

You have been a shelter for me, a strong tower from the enemy.
Psalm 61:3

MY PERSONAL PRAYER

*Security is not the absence of
danger, but the presence of God,
no matter what the danger.*
Author Unknown

Dear Father:

_____

_____

_____

_____

_____

_____

_____

Amen

God orders his angels to protect you wherever you go.
Psalm 91:11 NLT

*The Lord says, "I will rescue those who love me.
I will protect those who trust in my name."*
Psalm 91:14 NLT

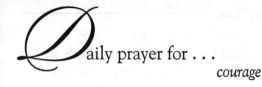
aily prayer for . . .

courage

> *Do not be afraid, nor be dismayed;*
> *be strong and of good courage.*
>
> Joshua 10:25

Heavenly Father,

I feel as if the sky could fall on me at any moment. Like Chicken Little, I want to run into a dark cave and hide away from my problems. I'd like to think that I'm a woman of courage, but right now, I'm not feeling strong or courageous.

Help me, Lord, to do the one thing I can do—stay close to You. After all, that's the first thing my children do when they're frightened. So . . . I come to You right now. I take hold of Your promise never to leave me. Chase away the shadows, I pray, and fill me with the courage that comes from Your presence.

Amen.

> *We are God's household, if we keep up our courage*
> *and remain confident in our hope in Christ.*
>
> Hebrews 3:6 NLT

MY PERSONAL PRAYER

Courage is not the absence of fear and despair, but the capacity to move forward, confidently trusting the Maker of the heavens to cover us with the shadow of His mighty hand, even if the sky should fall.

Susan Duke

Dear Father:

_____

_____

_____

_____

_____

_____

Amen

*Jesus spoke with them and said to them,
"Take courage; it is I, do not be afraid."*
Mark 6:50 NAS

*Be on guard. Stand true to what you believe.
Be courageous. Be strong.*
1 Corinthians 16:13 NLT

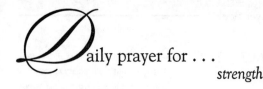

Daily prayer for . . .

strength

The Lord said to me, "My grace is sufficient for you, for My strength is made perfect in weakness."

2 Corinthians 12:9

Heavenly Father,

My children think I'm so strong. Oh yes, mother can do anything. You and I know that isn't the case. In fact, I'm a weakling and I need a lot of help—the kind only You can give. When I'm faithful to ask You to help me carry my burdens, motherhood seems doable again. I'm able to enjoy my children without worrying about every little problem.

Lord, I know how dependent I am on You. Believe me, I know. I'm grateful for Your help. You strengthen me physically, lift me up emotionally, empower me spiritually. You give me Your wisdom and understanding to deal with problems. You energize me with Your love.

It's really true, Lord. When I'm weak, You make me strong.

Amen.

God's weakness is far stronger than the greatest of human strength.
1 Corinthians 1:25 NLT

MY PERSONAL PRAYER

When I had reached the end of my ability to cope, God revealed himself as my strength and the love of my heart.

Heather Whitestone

Dear Father:

_____

_____

_____

_____

_____

_____

_____

Amen

*Never forget your promises to me your servant,
for they are my only hope. They give me strength in all
my troubles; how they refresh and revive me!*
Psalm 119:49 TLB

The Lord is the strength of my life; of whom shall I be afraid?
Psalm 27:1

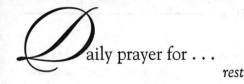

aily prayer for . . .

rest

> *Jesus said, "Come to Me, all you who labor*
> *and are heavy laden, and I will give you rest."*
> Matthew 11:28

Heavenly Father,

How do you take a day off from being a mother? This isn't like a regular job. My children need me around the clock. When I do have a chance to lie down for a few minutes, I feel guilty. There is just so much to do. On the other hand, if I don't rest, we all pay the price.

Show me those times during the day when I can slow down for a few minutes, take a break, rest. Though I know that even if I take advantage of each one, it won't be enough. So I ask You, Lord, to multiply those moments. Make those five-minute breaks feel like twenty or thirty minutes. Use those times to infuse me with Your strength. And I will give You my thanks.

Amen.

> *Rest in the Lord, and wait patiently for Him.*
> Psalm 37:7

MY PERSONAL PRAYER

*Lord, thou madest us for thyself,
and we can find no rest till we find
rest in thee.*

Saint Augustine

Dear Father:

_____

_____

_____

_____

_____

_____

Amen

My presence will go with you, and I will give you rest.
Exodus 33:14 RSV

*Jesus said, "Take My yoke upon you and learn from Me,
for I am gentle and lowly in heart, and you will find
rest for your souls."*
Matthew 11:29

Prayers to Encourage and Comfort the Soul   33

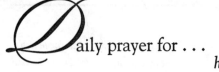

aily prayer for . . .
hope

*Let your unfailing love surround us, Lord, for
our hope is in you alone.*
Psalm 33:22 NLT

Heavenly Father,

Being a mother requires a lot of hope—hope that when
it's all said and done, I will have given my children
everything they need to succeed in life. Hope that they
will become good people, kind and caring. Hope that
they will live in peace and prosperity. And most of all,
hope that they will live in vital, living relationship with
You, their creator.

This world doesn't offer much hope, Lord. Some of my
friends have chosen not to have children because of the
conditions in which we all live. I respect their decisions,
but I see a better solution. I've chosen to place my hope
in You, Lord. I know I won't be disappointed.

Amen.

*Blessed is the man who trusts in the Lord and
has made the Lord his hope and confidence.*
Jeremiah 17:7 TLB

MY PERSONAL PRAYER

*"Hope" is the thing with feathers—
that perches in the soul. And sings
the tune without the words—and
never stops—at all.*

Emily Dickinson

Dear Father:

_____

_____

_____

_____

_____

_____

Amen

*I will hope continually, and will praise
You yet more and more.*
Psalm 71:14

*I wait for the Lord, my soul waits,
and in His word I do hope.*
Psalm 130:5

Prayers to Encourage and Comfort the Soul   35

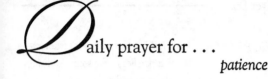

Daily prayer for . . .

patience

> *Let patience have its perfect work, that you*
> *may be perfect and complete, lacking nothing.*
> James 1:4

Heavenly Father,

We both know I'm not very good at being patient. I start out with the best of intentions—but very soon, I hear myself chiding my children, prodding them to move faster, do better. I realize that my failing causes problems for those I love, but I simply can't change without Your help.

I want to be kind and good to my children, rather than impatient and demanding. I want them to know each day that they are precious in Your eyes and in mine. Help me to be more like You, Lord. Teach me to be as patient and loving with my children as You were with the little ones who sat on Your knee.

Amen.

> *Patient endurance is what you need now, so you will continue to do*
> *God's will. Then you will receive all that he has promised.*
> Hebrews 10:36 NLT

MY PERSONAL PRAYER

Patience is a bitter plant but
it has a sweet fruit.
German Proverb

Dear Father:

_____

_____

_____

_____

_____

_____

Amen

Be glad for all God is planning for you.
Be patient in trouble, and always be prayerful.
Romans 12:12 NLT

Finishing is better than starting. Patience is better than pride.
Ecclesiastes 7:8 NLT

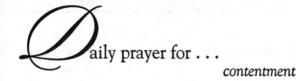

Daily prayer for . . .

contentment

I have learned in whatever state I am,
to be content.

Philippians 4:11

Heavenly Father,

I want to give my children the best life has to offer. But it seems like there is always something just outside my reach. Some toy. Some electronic gadget. Some trendy item of clothing.

Help me remember that there are so many more important things I can give my children—good values and faith for example. After all, I don't want them to become slaves to the material things of this world. Your provision has always been more than enough to meet our needs. Help me to teach my children to count their blessings, to have hearts filled with gratitude, and to see those things that are really important in life.

Amen.

Godliness with contentment is great gain.
1 Timothy 6:6

MY PERSONAL PRAYER

There is strength in contentment. It's not a dream stealer. You aren't required to settle. Contentment means that you have a peace about God's purpose for you right now.
David Edwards

Dear Father:

_____

_____

_____

_____

_____

_____

Amen

I know how to live on almost nothing or with everything. I have learned the secret of contentment in every situation, whether it be a full stomach or hunger, plenty or want.
Philippians 4:12 TLB

As for me, my contentment is not in wealth but in seeing you and knowing all is well between us.
Psalm 17:15 TLB

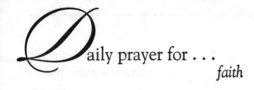

Daily prayer for . . .
faith

*I have prayed for you, that your faith
should not fail.*

Luke 22:32

Heavenly Father,

I'm not sure why, but it so much easier for me to have
faith for someone else's situation than for my own. I
pray for other moms and their children, and witness
victories. And yet, when I pray for my child, my faith
feels fragile.

Even when my faith feels weak, and I can't imagine how
You will work things out, give me confidence in Your
faithfulness. Help me remember the wonderful ways
You've stretched and developed my faith in the past. You
have answered every prayer and walked with me through
every difficulty. You've promised that even if my faith is
as tiny as a mustard seed, it is strong enough to move
mountains. Thank You for increasing my faith.

Amen.

*"If your faith were only the size of a mustard seed," Jesus answered,
"it would be large enough to uproot that mulberry tree over there
and send it hurtling into the sea!"*
Luke 17:6 TLB

MY PERSONAL PRAYER

Faith is not belief without proof,
but trust without reservations.
Elton Trueblood

Dear Father:

_____

_____

_____

_____

_____

_____

Amen

Jesus said, "Whatsoever things you ask in prayer,
believing, you will receive."
Matthew 21:22

The righteousness of God is revealed from faith to faith;
as it is written, "The just shall live by faith."
Romans 1:17

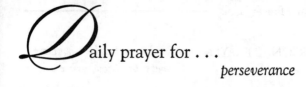

$\mathcal{D}$aily prayer for . . .

perseverance

> *You have heard of the perseverance of Job and*
> *seen the end intended by the Lord—that the*
> *Lord is very compassionate and merciful.*
>
> James 5:11

Heavenly Father,

We have a problem, and the road ahead looks long and arduous. I can't give up on my child, Lord. I have to see this through to the end. Refresh me with the promises from Your Word and the sweetness of Your Spirit. As I empty myself out before You, fill me again with the determination and the resolve to stay faithful to this commitment. Remind me that each day is a gift and an opportunity to move toward new goals and victories.

Please help me see this opportunity as a training ground used to develop character in me that is pleasing to You.

Amen.

> *We also glory in tribulations, knowing that tribulation produces*
> *perseverance; and perseverance, character; and character, hope.*
>
> Romans 5:3-4

MY PERSONAL PRAYER

When you get in a tight place and everything goes against you, till it seems you could not hold on a minute longer, never give up then, for that is just the place and time that the tide will turn.

Harriet Beecher Stowe

Dear Father:

_____

_____

_____

_____

_____

_____

Amen

Pay close attention to yourself and to your teaching; persevere in these things; for as you do this you will insure salvation both for yourself and for those who hear you.
1 Timothy 4:16 NAS

Don't get tired of doing what is good. Don't get discouraged and give up, for we will reap a harvest of blessing at the appropriate time.
Galatians 6:9 NLT

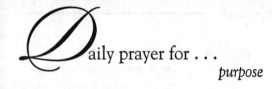 aily prayer for . . .

purpose

> *May He grant you according to your heart's
> desire, and fulfill all your purpose.*
>
> Psalm 20:4

Heavenly Father,

As I come to You with the desires of my heart, help me
evaluate the motives of my passion and purpose. Help
me to weed out cluttered thoughts, aimless pursuits,
and unattainable and unimportant goals. Help me
acknowledge and pursue those things that push me
toward Your plan for my life as a woman, wife, and
mother.

Establish Your goals in my heart and seal them with a
determined purpose to be what You created me to be.
Give me unselfish ambition. Guide and direct my
steps and help me guide my children onto the path of
purpose.

Amen.

> *Every purpose is established by counsel.*
> Proverbs 20:18 ASV

MY PERSONAL PRAYER

There is a path before you that you alone can walk. There is a purpose that you alone can fulfill.

Karla Dornacher

Dear Father:

_____

_____

_____

_____

_____

_____

Amen

We know that all things work together for good to those who love God, to those who are the called according to His purpose.
Romans 8:28

I run straight to the goal with purpose in every step. I fight to win. I'm not just shadow-boxing or playing around.
1 Corinthians 9:26 TLB

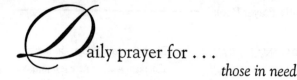

aily prayer for . . .

those in need

> *Yes, you will be enriched so that you can give
> even more generously. And when we take
> your gifts to those who need them, they will
> break out in thanksgiving to God.*
>
> 2 Corinthians 9:11 NLT

Heavenly Father,

So many people cross my path each day—people who
are in desperate need. I gladly give whatever and
whenever I can, but Father, my contribution feels like a
tiny grain of sand compared to the vastness of the
need. Show me how to do more—and bless more. Help
me instill the principle of giving from the heart in my
children, encouraging them to reach out as well.

Though we can do so little compared to the greater
need, You've proven time and again that You can turn
the little loaves and fishes of meager offerings into
abundance. Take what little we have to give; enrich
and multiply it. And we will be sure to give You all
the praise.

Amen.

> *If you give to the poor, your needs will be supplied!*
> Proverbs 28:27 TLB

MY PERSONAL PRAYER

No matter how little you have, you
can always give some of it away.
Catherine Marshall

Dear Father:

———————————————————

———————————————————

———————————————————

———————————————————

———————————————————

———————————————————

———————————————————

Amen

Jesus said, "God will give you all you need from day to day if
you make the Kingdom of God your primary concern."
Luke 12:31 NLT

The needy shall not always be forgotten.
Psalm 9:18

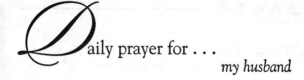

Daily prayer for . . .

my husband

*Wives, submit to your own husbands,
as to the Lord.*

Ephesians 5:22

Heavenly Father,

The children take up so much of my time. It seems like I have very little to devout to my husband. Help me carve out more time for him, offering the support and encouragement he needs. Help me demonstrate before my children the art of appreciation and the value of their father's dedication to us.

I know that valuing my husband is one of the best things I can do for my children. It helps them to feel secure in our home and open to interaction with their heavenly Father. Remind me not to nag, not to criticize, not to ridicule, but always to remember that You are making him the husband and father You created him to be.

Amen.

*That kind of deep beauty was seen in the saintly women of old,
who trusted God and fitted in with their husbands' plans.*

1 Peter 3:5 TLB

MY PERSONAL PRAYER

A good marriage is not a contract between two persons but a sacred covenant between three.
Donald Kaufman

Dear Father:

_____

_____

_____

_____

_____

_____

Amen

A man shall leave his father and mother and be joined to his wife, and they shall become one flesh.
Genesis 2:24

Give honor to marriage, and remain faithful to one another in marriage.
Hebrews 13:4 NLT

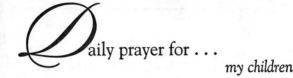

Daily prayer for . . .

my children

Children are a gift from the Lord.
Psalm 127:3 NLT

Heavenly Father,

From the very first moment I saw my children, I knew I'd been blessed with a miracle. Thank You for entrusting them to my care. It is a responsibility I cannot possibly handle on my own. Therefore, I call on You.

I pray that You would employ Your angels to watch over each one of them, guarding and protecting, keeping them from harm. And Father, close their ears to those words that could endanger their faith and sense of self-esteem. Keep them safe from the Evil One, I pray—the one who would strive to keep them from a relationship with You. And I will be certain to give You all the glory.

Amen.

May the Lord richly bless both you and your children.
Psalm 115:14 TLB

MY PERSONAL PRAYER

The mother's heart is the
child's schoolroom.
Henry Ward Beecher

Dear Father:

_____

_____

_____

_____

_____

_____

_____

Amen

The righteous walk in integrity;
happy are the children who follow them.
Proverbs 20:7 NRSV

The character of even a child can
be known by the way he acts.
Proverbs 20:11 TLB

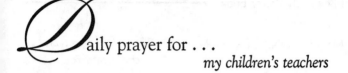

*D*aily prayer for . . .
my children's teachers

Teach me your ways, O Lord, that I may live according to your truth! Grant me purity of heart, that I may honor you.
Psalm 86:11 NLT

Heavenly Father,

Instructing and disciplining children all day long in a classroom must be a challenging task. I appreciate my children's teachers. Please bless them and the honorable position they hold. Help my children to be a blessing to their teachers as well.

Protect, guide, and help my children's teachers as they instill knowledge and skills into these young minds. Give them the grace and stamina they need while the children are in their care. Refresh them with the reward of knowing they are using their gifts to plant seeds of greatness. As they encourage, let them also be encouraged. As they teach, help them to also glean life lessons from the children in their care.

Amen.

Come, you children, listen to me; I will teach you the fear of the Lord.
Psalm 34:11

MY PERSONAL PRAYER

The art of teaching is the art of assisting discovery.

Mark Van Doren

Dear Father:

_____

_____

_____

_____

_____

_____

Amen

Teach Thou me what I do not see.
Job 34:32 NAS

*The wise man is known by his common sense,
and a pleasant teacher is the best.*
Proverbs 16:21 TLB

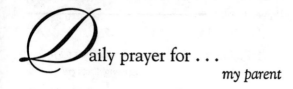

Daily prayer for . . .
my parent

Give your parents joy! May she who gave you birth be happy.
Proverbs 23:25 NLT

Heavenly Father,

Now that I'm a mom, I appreciate my mother more than ever before. I think about the hours she spent in prayer on my behalf. So it is with love and gratitude that I pray for her now. Bless her in the years ahead. Give her the blessing of seeing her children and grandchildren living happy, successful lives graced by Your presence. Give her the honor of seeing each one of us living in relationship with You.

When I was a child, I never gave much thought to the countless hours she cooked, cleaned, made sure I had clothes for school, read to me, and helped me recite my nightly prayers. But now, I can see that You greatly blessed me through her attitudes and actions. Bless and protect her now, I pray.

Amen.

Do not despise your mother when she is old.
Proverbs 23:22 NAS

MY PERSONAL PRAYER

*The family—that dear octopus
from whose tentacles we never
quite escape, nor, in our inmost
hearts, ever quite wish to.*
Dodie Smith

Dear Father:

_____

_____

_____

_____

_____

_____

Amen

*The righteous man walks in his integrity;
his children are blessed after him.*
Proverbs 20:7

Forsake not your mother's teaching.
Proverbs 6:20 RSV

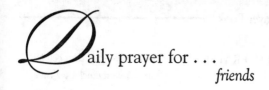

Daily prayer for . . .
friends

A friend loves at all times.

Proverbs 17:17

Heavenly Father,

I don't know what I'd do without my friends. I know many people as acquaintances, but there are only a handful of true friends that I would trust with my life. These are the friends that are like family. They've been with me through thick and thin. They're loyal and loving through every storm of life we've faced together.

As a mom I need friends who are also moms who understand the joys and the tribulations of motherhood. Thank you for friends who add such depth and dimension to my life. Let me not be slack in telling them how much they mean to me. Bless my friends with Your peace and provision. Most of all, heavenly Father, let me be the kind of friend to them that they've been to me.

Amen.

There are "friends" who destroy each other,
but a real friend sticks closer than a brother.
Proverbs 18:24 NLT

MY PERSONAL PRAYER

I didn't find my friends;
the good God gave them to me.
Ralph Waldo Emerson

Dear Father:

_____

_____

_____

_____

_____

_____

_____

Amen

The sweetness of a man's friend gives
delight by hearty counsel.
Proverbs 27:9

Jesus said, "Greater love has no one than this,
than to lay down one's life for his friends."
John 15:13

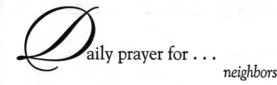

Daily prayer for . . .

neighbors

Jesus said, "You shall love your
neighbor as yourself."

Matthew 22:39

Heavenly Father,

Between carpooling, school meetings, family activities, and weekend schedules, there is little time left for getting to know my neighbors. It seems so different from when I was a child. Neighbors were always friends back then.

Heavenly Father, help me to be a better neighbor by stepping out and offering my hand in friendship. I don't want to intrude, but I can't help but wonder if they would like to know us as much as we would like to know them.

Show me ways to bless them, Lord, in word and in deed. And I promise to be listening. Even with all the activities in my life, I promise to respond to Your instructions.

Amen.

Better is a neighbor nearby than a brother far away.
Proverbs 27:10

MY PERSONAL PRAYER

*Only when one is connected
to one's own core, is one
connected to others.*
Anne Morrow Lindbergh

Dear Father:

_____

_____

_____

_____

_____

_____

Amen

You shall love your neighbor as yourself.
Leviticus 19:18

*Love does no harm to a neighbor;
therefore love is the fulfillment of the law.*
Romans 13:10

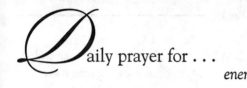

Daily prayer for . . .
enemies

> *Jesus said, "Pray for the happiness of those*
> *who curse you. Pray for those who hurt you."*
> Luke 6:28 NLT

Heavenly Father,

One of the hardest things You've asked me to do is pray for those who have hurt me, my child, or one of my family members. There have been times, I admit, that I haven't been willing to pray for my enemies. I wanted revenge, swift judgment, and an apology for their actions. But I've learned that too often an apology never comes, and I find myself locked into bitterness and unforgiveness.

Your word says that You are the vindicator, and that I am not to repay evil with evil. I trust You to deal justly and mercifully with them. And I will do my part, Lord. I will pray for the revelation of Your love in their lives. And with Your help, I will find the grace to forgive.

Amen.

If someone mistreats you because you are a Christian, don't curse him;
pray that God will bless him.
Romans 12:14 TLB

MY PERSONAL PRAYER

Pour not water on a
drowning mouse.

Thomas Fuller

Dear Father:

_____

_____

_____

_____

_____

_____

Amen

Jesus said, "Love your enemies, do good, and lend, hoping
for nothing in return; and your reward will be great."
Luke 6:35

God has shown you, O man, what is good; and what does
the Lord require of you but to do justly, to love mercy,
and to walk humbly with your God?
Micah 6:8

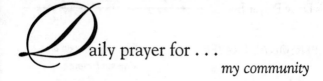

Daily prayer for . . .

my community

Make the most of your chances to tell others
the Good News. Be wise in all your contacts
with them.

Colossians 4:5 TLB

Heavenly Father,

My community is a special place—the place You've chosen for my children to be raised. Therefore, I lift this town and its citizens up to You. I ask that this would be a place where You are held in honor. I pray that our leaders would be Your chosen representatives and that their decisions would be pleasing in Your eyes.

Help me be supportive and willing to meet the needs that come to my attention. Keep me focused on being part of the solution and not part of the problems that often arise. Give me the grace to work with the others You've placed here to make our community a safe and godly home for our children.

Amen.

Let each of you look out not only for his own interests,
but also for the interests of others.
Philippians 2:4

MY PERSONAL PRAYER

We cannot live only for ourselves.
A thousand fibers connect us with
our fellow men.

Herman Melville

Dear Father:

_____

_____

_____

_____

_____

_____

_____

Amen

If we walk in the light as He is in the light, we have fellowship
with one another, and the blood of Jesus
1 John 1:7

Happiness comes to those who are fair to others
and are always just and good.
Psalm 106:3 TLB

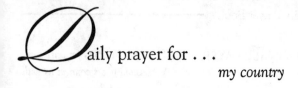

Daily prayer for . . .
my country

> *If My people who are called by My name will*
> *humble themselves, and pray and seek My*
> *face, and turn from their wicked ways, then I*
> *will hear from heaven, and will forgive their*
> *sin and heal their land.*
>
> 2 Chronicles 7:14

Heavenly Father,

I can't remember a time in history when our country
has been in greater need. Even our most basic beliefs
and the foundational values our country was founded
on are being called into question. Unless You intervene,
we may lose the freedoms so many have given so much
to protect.

We need You more than ever, Lord. Help me as a
mother and as a patriot stand for the things that will
affect the lives of my children and grandchildren. Keep
me mindful of the power in one vote, one voice, and
one action. I want to make a difference in my country
by making a difference first at home.

Amen.

The heavens declare his perfect righteousness; every nation sees his glory.
Psalm 97:6 TLB

MY PERSONAL PRAYER

*My country is the world;
my countrymen are mankind.*
William Lloyd Garrison

Dear Father:

_____

_____

_____

_____

_____

_____

Amen

*Lord, you know the hopes of humble people.
Surely you will hear their cries and comfort their hearts by helping them.*
Psalm 10:17 TLB

*Pray in this way for kings and all others who are in authority over us, or are
in places of high responsibility, so that we can live in peace and quietness,
spending our time in godly living and thinking much about the Lord.*
1 Timothy 2:2 TLB

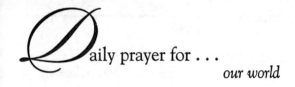

Daily prayer for . . .
our world

Heavenly Father,

Our world is a scary place to live. Each day, we read or hear of a new war breaking out somewhere. Cruelty heaped upon cruelty. Dictators, duplicity, hatred, and murder abound. As a mother, Lord, I believe that the only answer is the one the angel spoke of at the time of Your incarnation. That answer is peace.

Father, I pray for peace in the hearts of men and women and children around the world. Peace in the midst of chaos. Supernatural peace that shouts louder than tribal disputes, insane ambition, hatred, and war. Abiding peace that will allow us to prosper in this world until we are safely received into Your presence.

Amen.

MY PERSONAL PRAYER

*The unrest of this weary world is
its unvoiced cry after God.*
Theodore T. Munger

Dear Father:

_____

_____

_____

_____

_____

_____

Amen

*Your faithfulness endures to all generations;
You established the earth, and it abides.*
Psalm 119:90

*May the nations praise you, O God.
Yes, may all the nations praise you.*
Psalm 67:5 NLT

Prayers to Encourage and Comfort the Soul   67

Prayer is not conquering God's reluctance,
but taking hold of God's willingness.

Phillips Brooks

Daily Prayers for Help . . .

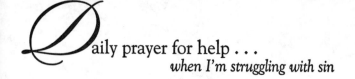

Daily prayer for help . . .
when I'm struggling with sin

In Him we have redemption through His
blood, the forgiveness of sins.

Ephesians 1:7

Heavenly Father,

It isn't obvious or deliberate sin I struggle with; it's the little sins that hinder my walk with You. When I seek tangible comfort instead of looking to You; when I rebel against Your will and try to do things my own way; when I ignore Your still, small voice of instruction and conviction; and when I my close my understanding to Your counsel, I open the door to sin.

Forgive me, Lord, for allowing life's daily struggles to harden my heart. Wash it clean. Soften it and make it pliable in Your hands. Keep my ears attuned to Your voice. And help me to be a better example for my children.

Amen.

If we confess our sins, He is faithful and just to forgive us
our sins and to cleanse us from all unrighteousness.
1 John 1:9

MY PERSONAL PRAYER

*Temptation provokes me to look
upward to God.*

John Bunyan

Dear Father:

_____

_____

_____

_____

_____

_____

_____

Amen

*You know that Jesus came to take away our sins,
for there is no sin in him. So if we continue to live in him,
we won't sin either.*
1 John 3:5-6 NLT

*This is real love. It is not that we loved God, but that he
loved us and sent his Son as a sacrifice to take away our sins.*
1 John 4:10 NLT

Prayers to Encourage and Comfort the Soul   71

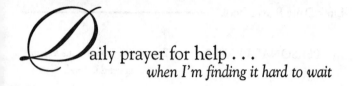

Daily prayer for help . . .
when I'm finding it hard to wait

> *Be still in the presence of the Lord, and wait*
> *patiently for him to act.*
>
> Psalm 37:7 NLT

Heavenly Father,

You know I have never been very good at waiting. I get restless and all too often run off in a state of panic to find my own solution. I'm certain that my failing is having an effect on my family, especially my children. And as I'm sure You know, my solutions almost always bring frustration and disappointment.

Lord, I ask You to work with me—and I'm asking boldly because I'm praying according to Your will. Teach me to wait patiently for Your answers, Your provisions, Your solutions. When I am tempted to run off on my own, restrain me by Your Spirit. I know our lives will be better because of it.

Amen.

> *Those who wait on the Lord shall renew their strength.*
> Isaiah 40:31

MY PERSONAL PRAYER

What a blessing when we wait on God who knows our heart's desires, and wants what is best for us and for those we love!

Nancy Corbett Cole

Dear Father:

_____

_____

_____

_____

_____

_____

Amen

I will wait for your mercies—for everyone knows what a merciful God you are.
Psalm 52:9 TLB

As your plan unfolds, even the simple can understand it. No wonder I wait expectantly for each of your commands.
Psalm 119:130-131 TLB

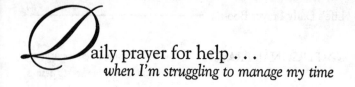

*D*aily prayer for help . . .
when I'm struggling to manage my time

> *Teach us to number our days, that we may*
> *gain a heart of wisdom.*
>
> Psalm 90:12

Heavenly Father,

I lay down each and every night with the same feeling—
that there just aren't enough hours in the day to do
everything. The anxiety that comes from trying to figure
it all out robs me of sleep and peace.

Lord, show me how to achieve a more balanced home
life for myself and my family. Show me where I might
be wasting precious time. What areas need to be
trimmed back so others can expand. As I review my
priorities, show me where changes need to be made.
Teach me, Lord, to value each second, each minute,
each hour, each day as a gift from You—a gift to be
used for Your glory.

Amen.

To everything there is a season, a time for every purpose under heaven.
Ecclesiastes 3:1

MY PERSONAL PRAYER

Lost yesterday, somewhere between sunrise and sunset, two golden hours, each set with sixty diamond minutes. No reward is offered, for they are gone forever.

Horace Mann

Dear Father:

_____

_____

_____

_____

_____

_____

Amen

Wisdom and knowledge will be the stability of your times, and the strength of salvation.
Isaiah 33:5

Walk circumspectly, not as fools but as wise, redeeming the time, because the days are evil.
Ephesians 5:15-16

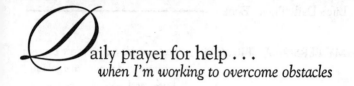

Daily prayer for help . . .
when I'm working to overcome obstacles

> *By You I can run against a troop; by my God
> I can leap over a wall.*
>
> 2 Samuel 22:30

Heavenly Father,

I want to do the things that You are asking of me, but there are so many obstacles in the way. It seems like everywhere I turn, I'm crashing into a brick wall. I need Your power and Your discernment to get where You want me to go.

Lord, I ask You to show me that little hole where I can wiggle through, the space where I can crawl under or over or around. Even when things look hopeless, I know that You will make a way. And I pray that as You do, You will open my children's eyes so that they will see that You are a God of miracles—a God who is ready to help them overcome the obstacles in their lives.

Amen.

> *O Sovereign Lord! You have made the heavens
> and earth by your great power. Nothing is too hard for you!*
> Jeremiah 32:17 NLT

MY PERSONAL PRAYER

Success is to be measured not so much by the position that one has reached in life as by the obstacles which he has overcome while trying to succeed.
Booker T. Washington

Dear Father:

_____

_____

_____

_____

_____

_____

Amen

In your strength I can scale any wall, attack any troop.
Psalm 18:29 TLB

*God trains my hands for battle,
so that my arms can bend a bow of bronze.*
2 Samuel 22:35 NAS

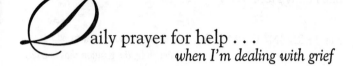

Daily prayer for help . . .
when I'm dealing with grief

> *Hear my prayer, O Lord, and give ear to my*
> *cry; hold not thy peace at my tears!*
>
> Psalm 39:12 RSV

Heavenly Father,

I'm worried about my children. They can't help but see my grief and sense that I'm hurting, no matter how I might try to hide it from them. And maybe I shouldn't try to do that anyway. I don't want to pretend, or stuff my feelings away, ignoring what's going on inside. Help me to process this grief in the right way and show my children that life's seasons bring us loss—but loss graced by new beginnings.

Walk with me along this lonely path, Lord. Shine Your light upon my darkness. Wrap me in a blanket of Your comfort and love while You are restoring and healing my heart. And let my children see Your tender mercy and grace being poured out on me. Let them see that You are there for us—even in the darkest places of our lives.

Amen.

> *Those who sow in tears shall reap in joy.*
>
> Psalm 126:5

MY PERSONAL PRAYER

*God makes a way even through
death and suffering by revealing
his presence.*

Dr. Henry Cloud

Dear Father:

_____

_____

_____

_____

_____

_____

Amen

O Lord, have mercy on me in my anguish.
Psalm 31:9 TLB

*You have seen me tossing and turning through the night. You
have collected all my tears and preserved them in your bottle!
You have recorded every one in your book.*
Psalm 56:8 TLB

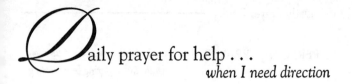

Daily prayer for help . . .
when I need direction

*A man's heart plans his way, but the Lord
directs his steps.*

Proverbs 16:9

Heavenly Father,

I'm a grown-up. Seems like I should know where I'm
going by now, what to do in certain situations, how to
make good choices and wise decisions—but way too
often, I don't. I need You to speak to me, perhaps
through my circumstances or a wise person who crosses
my path. I'll search Your Word for the answer, Lord.
And I'll listen carefully for Your voice speaking in the
stillness of my heart.

I place myself purposefully in the way of Your counsel,
trusting that You will direct me as I search for the path
You've prepared for me. I know, Lord, that my family
will be affected by my choices, so I dare not make them
without You. As I go on my way, I will be watching and
listening for Your voice.

Amen.

*The Lord, your Redeemer, the Holy One of Israel, says: "I am the Lord
your God, who teaches you what is good and leads you along the paths
you should follow"*
Isaiah 48:17 NLT

MY PERSONAL PRAYER

The Christian journey is the process of learning to accept Christ's outstretched hand as He leads us down the sometimes mucky road of life.

Leslie Williams

Dear Father:

_____

_____

_____

_____

_____

_____

Amen

*Many are the plans in the mind of a man,
but it is the purpose of the Lord that will be established.*
Proverbs 19:21 RSV

*In all your ways acknowledge Him,
and He shall direct your paths.*
Proverbs 3:6

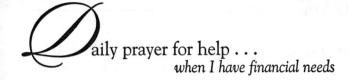

$\mathcal{D}$aily prayer for help . . .
when I have financial needs

> *I have never seen the Lord forsake a man who*
> *loves him; nor have I seen the children of the*
> *godly go hungry.*
>
> Psalm 37:25 TLB

Heavenly Father,

You know the challenges we are facing in our
finances—I don't need to go over them all again.
Instead, I'm here because Your Word says that if we ask,
we will receive. I'm asking for Your provision—and for
Your peace and patience until it comes.

I acknowledge Your power in this situation, and I've
witnessed Your faithfulness time after time. I know
that You will not let us down. You will not allow my
children to do without the things they need. You will
make a way where there is no way. You will provide.
And Lord, I thank You for it even before the answer
comes because You have never EVER failed to keep
Your promises.

Amen.

> *I want you to trust me in your times of trouble,*
> *so I can rescue you and you can give me glory.*
> Psalm 50:15 TLB

MY PERSONAL PRAYER

*True abundance is not about gathering
more things, it's about touching the place
in us that is connected to the divine source
of abundance, so that we know what we
need in the moment will be provided.*

Mary Manin Morrissey

Dear Father:

_____

_____

_____

_____

_____

_____

Amen

*Jesus said, "What man is there among you who, if his son
asks for bread, will give him a stone?"*
Matthew 7:9

*You shall remember the Lord your God, for it is He who gives
you power to get wealth, that He may establish His covenant
which He swore to your fathers, as it is this day.*
Deuteronomy 8:18

Prayers to Encourage and Comfort the Soul   83

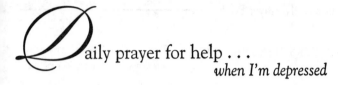

Daily prayer for help . . .
when I'm depressed

From the end of the earth will I call unto thee,
when my heart is overwhelmed: Lead me to
the rock that is higher than I.

Psalm 61:2 ASV

Heavenly Father,

I know it's not Your will for me to feel this way, but I can't seem to shake this depression that has settled like heavy fog over my soul. If I could help myself I would. All I can do is come to You and ask You to see me through this time.

Renew my mind, Lord. Whisper a song to my heart once again. Speak to me through Your word and refresh my spirit. I want to protect my children from this darkness. They are my greatest joy in this life, and joy is what they need from me. In the Psalms, David cried out to You. You answered him and delivered him from his despairing thoughts. Father, You are not a respecter of persons. What you did for David, I believe You will do for me. Even in this lonely place, I believe—You are near.

Amen.

We are pressed on every side by troubles, but not crushed and broken.
We are perplexed because we don't know why things happen as they do,
but we don't give up and quit.

2 Corinthians 4:8 TLB

MY PERSONAL PRAYER

*I can allow the light of His life and
love to shine through me,
or I can turn away and sit
in the murky stillness of
my disillusionment.*

Marilyn Meberg

Dear Father:

_____

_____

_____

_____

_____

_____

Amen

*Even when walking through the dark valley of death
I will not be afraid, for you are close beside me, guarding,
guiding all the way.*
Psalm 23:4 TLB

*God has redeemed my soul in peace from the battle
that was against me.*
Psalm 55:18

Prayers to Encourage and Comfort the Soul   85

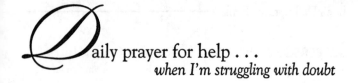

aily prayer for help . . .
when I'm struggling with doubt

*Jesus said, "Blessed are those who
don't doubt me."*
Matthew 11:6 TLB

Heavenly Father,

I don't understand where all this doubt is coming from.
I've read about Your faithfulness in Your Word so many
times. I've witnessed Your power in my life and in the
lives of my husband and children. I believe You are
always working in our circumstances, even when I can't
see what You're doing.

I want to believe without a shadow of a doubt. I want
my doubts and fears to be replaced with faith and hope.
In the same unspoiled way that my children trust me, I
want to trust You. I ask You for the same mercy You
showed Thomas and the brethren when they doubted
that You were indeed alive from the dead. In the midst
of my doubt, Lord, help me believe.

Amen.

*Let us hold fast the confession of our hope without wavering,
for He who promised is faithful.*
Hebrews 10:23

MY PERSONAL PRAYER

Kill the snake of doubt in your soul, crush the worms of fear in your heart and mountains will move out of your way.

Kate Seredy

Dear Father:

_____

_____

_____

_____

_____

_____

Amen

But let him ask in faith, with no doubting, for he who doubts is like a wave of the sea driven and tossed by the wind.
James 1:6

Jesus said, "Do not be afraid; only believe."
Mark 5:36

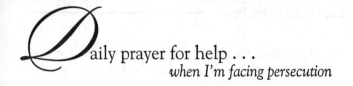

$\mathcal{D}$aily prayer for help . . .
when I'm facing persecution

> *Jesus said, "God blesses you when you are*
> *mocked and persecuted and lied about because*
> *you are my followers."*
> Matthew 5:11 NLT

Heavenly Father,

I don't even want to think about the consequences of the stand I've taken. I took the narrow road—the unpopular path. I followed my heart; I was obedient to the task You assigned to me. I anticipated that my words and actions would bring persecution, and they have. Now I ask that You give me Your grace to endure it, so that I can show my children the value of doing what is right and good, regardless of criticism.

And when I feel the prickly jabs, remind me that my puny sacrifice is nothing compared to the persecution You endured on the cross. And yet, You chose to forgive. Fill my heart with forgiveness for those who are persecuting me.

Amen.

Being reviled, we bless; being persecuted, we endure.
1 Corinthians 4:12

MY PERSONAL PRAYER

*God can take your trouble and
turn it into treasure.*

Barbara Johnson

Dear Father:

_____

_____

_____

_____

_____

_____

Amen

*Yes, and all who desire to live godly in
Christ Jesus will suffer persecution.*
2 Timothy 3:12

*Jesus said, "Blessed are you when they revile
and persecute you, and say all kinds of evil against you
falsely for My sake."*
Matthew 5:11

Prayers to Encourage and Comfort the Soul   89

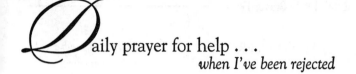

Daily prayer for help . . .
when I've been rejected

*But this happened that the word might be
fulfilled which is written in their law, "They
hated me without a cause."*

John 15:25

Heavenly Father,

I wish it weren't true, but we human beings base our
value much too often on other's opinions. I think I'm in
the majority of people who can receive ten compliments
or affirmations, and one negative comment, and only
dwell on the negative.

Lord, I know that rejection is part of life. I teach my
children that it doesn't matter what other people say. As
long as they know I love them, and You love them, that's
all that matters. It's hard to take my own advice at times.
Rejection hurts. It makes me feel unworthy and inadequate.
Help me remember that even rejection can make me
stronger. Strengthen my fragile spirit by remembering
that my true worth and value comes from You.

Amen.

*The eyes of the Lord watch over those who do right;
his ears are open to their cries for help.*
Psalm 34:15 NLT

MY PERSONAL PRAYER

When one door is shut,
another opens.

Cervantes

Dear Father:

——————————————————————

——————————————————————

——————————————————————

——————————————————————

——————————————————————

——————————————————————

Amen

Humble yourselves under the mighty hand of God,
that He may exalt you in due time.
1 Peter 5:6

Uphold me according to Your word, that I may live;
and do not let me be ashamed of my hope.
Psalm 119:116

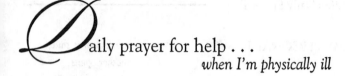

Daily prayer for help . . .
when I'm physically ill

> *The Lord will strengthen him on his bed of illness; you will sustain him on his sickbed.*
>
> Psalm 41:3

Heavenly Father,

Your Word reveals that You are not a respecter of people—and that what You have done for others, You can and will do for me. I believe in Your power to heal me from this sickness. I ask You to strengthen me and restore my health.

Lord, I realize You use doctors to administer healing; but I've been to the doctors and they haven't helped. But You are the Great Physician, the ultimate source of all healing. I take You at Your word, remembering with a thankful heart that You bore the stripes for my healing on the cross. You are the only one who can make me whole. Therefore, I will trust in Your mercy and grace.

Amen.

> *Beloved, I pray that all may go well with you and that you may be in health; I know that it is well with your soul.*
>
> 3 John 1:2 RSV

MY PERSONAL PRAYER

Health is more valuable
than wealth. . .
LeRoy Brownlow

Dear Father:

_____

_____

_____

_____

_____

_____

Amen

The prayer of faith will save the sick,
and the Lord will raise him up.
James 5:15

O Lord my God, I cried out to You, and You healed me.
Psalm 30:2

Prayers to Encourage and Comfort the Soul   93

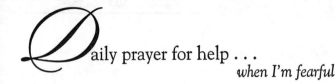

Daily prayer for help . . .

when I'm fearful

We will not fear, even though the earth be
removed, and though the mountains be carried
into the midst of the sea.

Psalm 46:2

Heavenly Father,

I'm afraid—too much, too often. And I'm afraid that
I'm teaching my children to be fearful as well. I need
Your help!

Give me the discernment I need to identify those areas
where fear has taken hold of me. Then, Lord, I pray
that You would help me place all that fear at Your feet
and leave it there. Free me to trust that You will protect
me and those I love. I know that You will show me
when I need to be cautious, and when I am allowing
fear to take charge. I thank You for helping me
exchange my fears for faith, and my hesitation with
boldness.

Amen.

You shall not be afraid of the terror by night,
nor of the arrow that flies by day.

Psalm 91:5

MY PERSONAL PRAYER

*Set your thoughts,
not on the storm, but on the love
that rules the storm.*
Mrs. Charles E. Cowman

Dear Father:

_____

_____

_____

_____

_____

_____

Amen

*We can say with confidence, "The Lord is my helper, so I
will not be afraid. What can mere mortals do to me?"*
Hebrews 13:6 NLT

*There is no fear in love; but perfect love casts out fear,
because fear involves torment. But he who fears has not been
made perfect in love.*
1 John 4:18

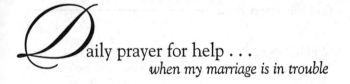

Daily prayer for help . . .
when my marriage is in trouble

*Trouble and anguish have come upon me, but
thy commandments are my delight.*
Psalm 119:143 RSV

Heavenly Father,

My husband and I have allowed the pressures and stress
of this life to steal the joy and intimacy we once had in
our marriage. It seems like lately we've lost touch with
each other, simply going through the motions.

I pray, Lord, that You would repair the breeches in our
marriage. Help me to put my own concerns aside and
focus on being a better wife to my husband. Rekindle
the flame of love between us. And help us to remember
that our children need us—together in body and soul.
We are their security, their first line of defense. As we
have vowed before You to love each other, give us now
Your grace to keep that vow.

Amen.

*He shall call upon Me, and I will answer him;
I will be with him in trouble; I will deliver him and honor him.*
Psalm 91:15

MY PERSONAL PRAYER

The truest joys they seldom prove,
Who free from quarrels live; 'tis the
most tender part of love, Each
other to forgive.
John Sheffield, Duke of Buckingham

Dear Father:

_____

_____

_____

_____

_____

_____

                                    Amen

God is our refuge and strength, a very present help in trouble.
Psalm 46:1

In the day of my trouble I sought the Lord.
Psalm 77:2 NAS

Prayers to Encourage and Comfort the Soul   97

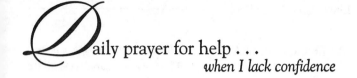

$\mathcal{D}$aily prayer for help . . .
when I lack confidence

> *Being confident of this very thing, that He*
> *who has begun a good work in you will*
> *complete it until the day of Jesus Christ.*
> Philippians 1:6

Heavenly Father,

In the past, I've had faith in my own abilities, believing I could handle anything life threw my way. I've learned from that false sense of security that plans fail, people disappoint, and at times I even let myself down. Life's experiences have shown me that I can't always depend on or expect my self-efforts to accomplish anything lasting.

Now that I'm a mom, I have a much clearer picture of confidence. I often see more confidence in my children than I do in myself. Could it be because they are confident that I will help them? Teach me how to trust You in the way my children trust me. for You are the way-maker, the gift-giver, and the security I need to accomplish all things. Thank You for the kind of steadfast confidence that comes from knowing You.

Amen.

The Lord will be your confidence, and will keep your foot from being caught.
Proverbs 3:26

MY PERSONAL PRAYER

Be like the bird, who halting in his flight on a limb too slight feels it give way beneath him, And yet sings knowing he hath wings.

Victor Hugo

Dear Father:

_____

_____

_____

_____

_____

_____

Amen

We have become partakers of Christ if we hold the beginning of our confidence steadfast to the end.
Hebrews 3:14

Blessed is the man who trusts in the Lord and has made the Lord his hope and confidence.
Jeremiah 17:7 TLB

Prayers to Encourage and Comfort the Soul   99

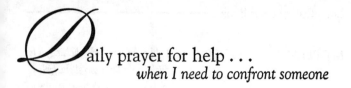

Daily prayer for help . . .
when I need to confront someone

Open rebuke is better than love carefully concealed.
Proverbs 27:5

Heavenly Father,

Everything in me wants to run and hide. It isn't easy to confront someone. But I know that resolution cannot come until the problem is addressed.

I don't know how this situation will turn out, Lord. But I ask You for the boldness and honesty to speak the truth with conviction, and the meekness to speak the truth in love. My prayer is that by facing up to my responsibility, this situation will be stripped of its power to do harm and the relationship will once again prosper. I release any anger and resentment, and I ask that You will help me present myself in a way that is pleasing to You.

One day, Lord, when my children face such a situation, I want to be able to tell them with confidence that You will see them through as they, too, do the difficult thing.

Amen.

Jesus said, "If another believer sins against you, go privately and point out the fault. If the other person listens and confesses it, you have won that person back."
Matthew 18:15 NLT

MY PERSONAL PRAYER

No legacy is so rich as honesty.
Shakespeare

Dear Father:

_____

_____

_____

_____

_____

_____

Amen

*It is better to hear the rebuke of the wise than
for a man to hear the song of fools.*
Ecclesiastes 7:5

Those who deal truthfully are God's delight.
Proverbs 12:22 NKJV

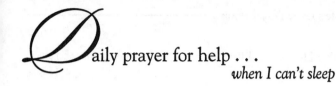

$\mathcal{D}$aily prayer for help . . .
when I can't sleep

God gives His beloved sleep.
Psalm 127:2

Heavenly Father,

I've lost count of my sleepless nights. Nothing I've tried
has helped: counting sheep, drinking warm milk, or
reading. I've searched myself, wondering what it is that
could be keeping me awake, but so far, I haven't found
the answer.

Lord, I ask You to reveal to me what it is I haven't been
able to see. If it's anxiety, I ask that You help me lay it
aside. If it's hidden sin, I ask You to expose it so that I
can be cleansed and forgiven. If You are waking me to
pray, then show me how I can be obedient to You. I
place myself in Your loving care—completely and
without hesitation. As I close my eyes, help me to find
what I so badly need—blessed sleep.

Amen.

*When you lie down, you will not be afraid; yes,
you will lie down and your sleep will be sweet.*
Proverbs 3:24

MY PERSONAL PRAYER

*Every evening I turn my worries
over to God. He's going to be up
all night anyway.*

Mary C. Crowley

Dear Father:

_____

_____

_____

_____

_____

_____

Amen

*I will both lie down in peace, and sleep; for You alone,
O Lord, make me dwell in safety.*
Psalm 4:8

I lie down and sleep; I wake again, for the Lord sustains me.
Psalm 3:5 RSV

Prayers to Encourage and Comfort the Soul   103

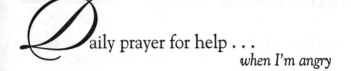

Daily prayer for help . . .
when I'm angry

A hot-tempered man stirs up strife, but he
who is slow to anger quiets contention.
Proverbs 15:18 RSV

Heavenly Father,

I don't mean to let anger get the best of me, but so
often that's exactly what I do. It's time for me to
acknowledge what You've known all along—I can't
handle my anger by myself. I desperately need Your
help, Lord. And I'm ready to submit myself—my anger,
my attitude, all of myself—to You.

I want my children to be raised in a home filled with
peace. I know that can only happen as Your Spirit rules
and reigns in our hearts and in our lives. Begin with my
heart, my life, Lord. Expose those unhealthy emotions
that I've been protecting and help me fill the space
where anger once overwhelmed me with faith and
hope.

Amen.

The fruit of the Spirit is love, joy, peace, longsuffering, kindness, goodness,
faithfulness, gentleness, self-control. Against such there is no law.
Galatians 5:22-23

MY PERSONAL PRAYER

*You can not acquire the gift of
peace if by your anger you destroy
the peace of the Lord.*

Gregory the Great

Dear Father:

_____

_____

_____

_____

_____

_____

Amen

*A soft answer turns away wrath,
but a harsh word stirs up anger.*
Proverbs 15:1

*The fruit of righteousness is sown in peace
by those who make peace.*
James 3:18

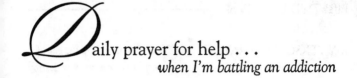

Daily prayer for help . . .
when I'm battling an addiction

The temptations that come into your life are no different from what others experience. And God is faithful. He will keep the temptation from becoming so strong that you can't stand up against it. When you are tempted, he will show you a way out so that you will not give in to it.
1 Corinthians 10:13 NLT

Heavenly Father,

During a season of weakness, I lost sight of Your peace and direction. I sought counterfeit comfort and immediate solace instead of seeking You. Now, I find myself bound in a way I never planned or expected.

I know that I must take responsibility for my recovery, but I also know that I can't break free without Your help. Give me the strength I need to find wholeness and light, one hour, one minute, one impulse at a time.

My children need me, Lord. They need a mother who is whole and healthy and overflowing with Your love. Thank You for helping me find the way to freedom.

Amen.

The Lord God will help Me; therefore I will not be disgraced; therefore I have set my face like a flint, and I know that I will not be ashamed.
Isaiah 50:7

MY PERSONAL PRAYER

My ability to be an instrument of God's grace is limited by my willingness to be an object of God's grace. The degree to which I allow my ugliness to be revealed to Him is the degree to which His beauty will be revealed in me.

Dan Christensen

Dear Father:

_____

_____

_____

_____

_____

_____

Amen

Jesus said, "Watch and pray, lest you enter into temptation. The spirit indeed is willing, but the flesh is weak."
Matthew 26:41

They will come to their senses and escape from Satan's trap of slavery to sin, which he uses to catch them whenever he likes, and then they can begin doing the will of God.
2 Timothy 2:26 TLB

Prayers to Encourage and Comfort the Soul   107

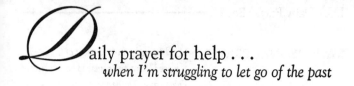

*D*aily prayer for help . . .
when I'm struggling to let go of the past

I do not count myself to have apprehended; but
one thing I do, forgetting those things which are
behind and reaching forward to those things
which are ahead, I press toward the goal for the
prize of the upward call of God in Christ Jesus.
Philippians 3:13-14

Heavenly Father,

I remember the day I laid down my old ways and began a
new walk with You. You've delivered me, forgiven me,
and accepted me. That's why I'm certain it isn't Your
voice I hear reminding me of who I used to be, tearing me
down, poking holes in my faith. Help me resist the voice
of the accuser. Renew my mind daily with Your promises.

Lord, help me to act swiftly when my thoughts return to
the past, turning my focus to the Holy Spirit. With
each victory, re-enforce my ability to live in the light of
today, being the best mother, the best person, the best
Child of God that I can possibly be.

Amen.

The unfailing love of the Lord never ends! By his mercies we have been
kept from complete destruction. Great is his faithfulness; his mercies begin
afresh each day.
Lamentations 3:22-23 NLT

MY PERSONAL PRAYER

I have no yesterdays, time took them away; tomorrow may not be—but I have today.
Pearl Yeadon McGinnis

Dear Father:

_____

_____

_____

_____

_____

_____

_____

Amen

The winter is past, the rain is over and gone.
Song of Songs 2:11

God has put a new song in my mouth.
Psalm 40:3

The purpose of all prayer is to find God's will and to make that will our prayer.

Catherine Marshall

Daily Prayers for Guidance . . .

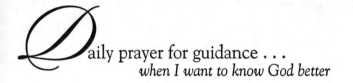

*D*aily prayer for guidance . . .
when I want to know God better

*As the deer pants for the water brooks, so
pants my soul for You, O God.*

Psalm 42:1

Heavenly Father,

I'm no longer satisfied with just knowing about You. I
want to know You intimately as my friend, my counselor,
and my provider. Lead me into a deeper place with You.
Take me into the Holy of Holies where I can feel Your
presence and share the secrets of my heart.

Give me a deep, abiding joy that flows from Your spirit.
Strengthen my walk, my ways, and my skills as a mother
and woman of God. As I empty myself out before You,
fill me each day with Your vision and purpose for my
life.

My heart is thirsty for You, Lord. Make it Your sanctuary
and our meeting place.

Amen.

Jesus said, "If anyone is thirsty, let him come to me and drink."
John 7:37 TLB

MY PERSONAL PRAYER

*Do not have your concert first and
tune your instruments afterwards.
Begin the day with God.*

James Hudson Taylor

Dear Father:

_____

_____

_____

_____

_____

_____

Amen

*Search me, O God, and know my heart; test my thoughts.
Point out anything you find in me that makes you sad, and
lead me along the path of everlasting life.*
Psalm 139:23-24 TLB

*I reach out for you. I thirst for you as
parched land thirsts for rain.*
Psalm 143:6 TLB

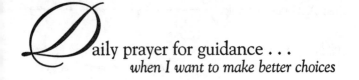

Daily prayer for guidance . . .
when I want to make better choices

> *Where is the man who fears the Lord? God*
> *will teach him how to choose the best. He*
> *shall live within God's circle of blessing, and*
> *his children shall inherit the earth.*
>
> Psalm 25:12-13 TLB

Heavenly Father,

I acknowledge You as the Source of all wisdom. I confess that Your ways are superior to my own. Forgive me for all the times when I've moved ahead and left You out of choices that impact my family. I've come to see just how important Your guidance is in my life.

That's why I'm ready to surrender my will to Yours. I know that doing so will clear the water, allowing me to see to the depths of a situation. No longer will my children have to suffer with the consequences of my selfishness and shortsightedness.

As I come before You, Lord, I ask You to meet me. Open my eyes to Your wisdom and truth and lead me in Your ways.

Amen.

> *Guide me with your laws so that I will not be overcome by evil.*
> Psalm 119:133 TLB

MY PERSONAL PRAYER

*God offers to every mind its choice
between truth and repose.*
Ralph Waldo Emerson

Dear Father:

_____

_____

_____

_____

_____

_____

Amen

*I have set before you life and death, blessing and cursing;
therefore choose life that both you and your
descendants may live.*
Deuteronomy 30:19

Let us choose what is right.
Job 34:4 RSV

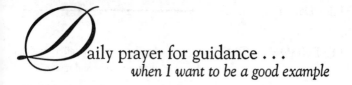

Daily prayer for guidance . . .
when I want to be a good example

You yourself must be an example to them of good deeds of every kind. Let everything you do reflect your love of the truth and the fact that you are in dead earnest about it.

Titus 2:7 TLB

Heavenly Father,

It's so easy to forget that my children are always watching, learning about life from my actions. Setting a proper example for them is a huge responsibility—one I know I can't carry without Your help.

Lord, I ask You to stop me in my tracks when I do or say something that dishonors You. Too well I realize that those times will come no matter how hard I wish to strip them from my life. Give me an opportunity to ask for Your forgiveness and then for theirs when my example has been compromised. And help them to see through my frailties to the example set by Your Son— the ever-faithful one.

Amen.

For this reason I obtained mercy, that in me first Jesus Christ might show all longsuffering, as a pattern to those who are going to believe on Him for everlasting life.
1 Timothy 1:16

MY PERSONAL PRAYER
Blessed is the influence on one true,
loving human soul on another.
George Eliot

Dear Father:

_____

_____

_____

_____

_____

_____

Amen

Jesus said, "I have given you an example to follow:
do as I have done to you."
John 13:15 TLB

Jesus said, "Good salt is worthless if it loses its saltiness;
it can't season anything. So don't lose your flavor!
Live in peace with each other."
Mark 9:50 TLB

Prayers to Encourage and Comfort the Soul   117

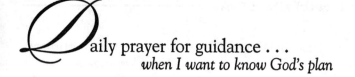

Daily prayer for guidance . . .
when I want to know God's plan

*I know the plans I have for you," says the
Lord. "They are plans for good and not for
evil, to give you a future and a hope.*
Jeremiah 29:11 TLB

Heavenly Father,

I believe that You have a wonderful plan for my life—a
plan far more exciting and fulfilling and productive than
any I could map out for myself. Still I've been known
to make my own plans without giving the slightest
consideration to how they will fit into Your master plan.

Lord, I want to leave that bad habit behind. I want to
begin to pursue YOUR plan, YOUR timing. I want to
set my feet on the path to becoming all that You have
called me to be. It's the only way that I can become the
best possible mother, the best possible wife, the best
possible friend, the best possible employee, the best
possible ME. It's the only way that I can bring honor
and glory to You. Show me Your plan, Lord—one step
at a time.

Amen.

*Your eyes saw my substance, being yet unformed. And in Your
book they all were written, the days fashioned for me,
when as yet there were none of them.*
Psalm 139:16

MY PERSONAL PRAYER

The strength of a man consists in finding out the way in which God is going, and going in that way too.
Henry Ward Beecher

Dear Father:

_____

_____

_____

_____

_____

_____

Amen

The steps of a good man are ordered by the Lord, and He delights in his way.
Psalm 37:23

O God, You are my God; early will I seek You; my soul thirsts for You; my flesh longs for You in a dry and thirsty land where there is no water.
Psalm 63:1

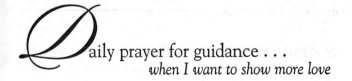

Daily prayer for guidance . . .
when I want to show more love

*Above all things have fervent love for
one another, for "love will cover a
multitude of sins."*

1 Peter 4:8

Heavenly Father,

If it weren't for You, I would not even be capable of
love, not for myself and certainly not for others. But the
fact is that You loved me first. You reached out to me
when I was helpless and made me love-*able*. What a gift
of grace.

I ask, Lord, that You would open my eyes to opportunities
to let You love others through me. Each time I hug my
children, let them feel Your love flowing through me.
Allow me to give away Your love freely, lavishly just as it
was given to me. I want to be Your conduit of love to all
those in my world. Thank You for the privilege.

Amen.

*Beloved, let us love one another, for love is of God; and everyone who
loves is born of God and knows God. He who does not love does not
know God, for God is love.*
1 John 4:7-8

MY PERSONAL PRAYER

*Where there is great love
there are miracles.*

Willa Cather

Dear Father:

_____

_____

_____

_____

_____

_____

Amen

*I pray that your love may abound still more and more in
knowledge and all discernment, that you may approve the
things that are excellent, that you may be sincere and without
offense till the day of Christ.*
Philippians 1:9-10

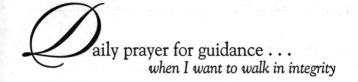

Daily prayer for guidance . . .
when I want to walk in integrity

The integrity of the upright will guide them,
but the perversity of the unfaithful will
destroy them.

Proverbs 11:3

Heavenly Father,

I see it all around us—lying, cheating, dishonesty. It's like seeing a flood sweep through the streets, uncontrollable, dangerous, leaving everything in its path damaged and dirty. I know how important it is for me to model the values of honesty, truthfulness, honor, and fidelity before my children. It's like giving them a tree to cling to as the flood waters pass by.

But we both know, Lord, that I am not capable of walking perfectly in this life. I ask first of all that You would expose any area of my life that lacks integrity, any place where the flood waters have seeped through. Give me insight, understanding, and the courage to make things right. I thank You for it, my Redeemer and my Lord.

Amen.

He who walks with integrity walks securely,
but he who perverts his ways will become known.
Proverbs 10:9

MY PERSONAL PRAYER

Integrity without knowledge is weak and useless, and knowledge without integrity is dangerous and dreadful.
Samuel Johnson

Dear Father:

_____

_____

_____

_____

_____

_____

Amen

Let integrity and uprightness preserve me.
Psalm 25:21

*As for me, You uphold me in my integrity,
And set me before Your face forever.*
Psalm 41:12

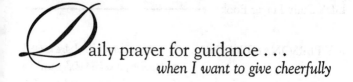

Daily prayer for guidance . . .
when I want to give cheerfully

Let each one give as he purposes in his heart,
not grudgingly or of necessity; for God loves a
cheerful giver.

2 Corinthians 9:7

Heavenly Father,

You've given so much to me. And You gave it freely, sacrificially, always looking out for my good. I want to be that kind of giver. I want to teach my children how to give in that way. But I find it's still a struggle. My heart says "give" but my hand says "keep" and my mind bounces back and forth between the two.

Lord, I ask that You would infuse me with the joy of giving. Make it my passion, something I can't wait to do. Settle the battle in my mind by giving me just the smallest glimpse of what You gave to me on the cross. Loosen my hand to be an instrument of Your blessing and provision. Take my desire to do what is right and make of me a cheerful giver.

Amen.

Let each of you look out not only for his own interests,
but also for the interests of others.
Philippians 2:4

MY PERSONAL PRAYER

There is no happiness in having or in getting, but only in giving.
Henry Drummond

Dear Father:

———————————————————

———————————————————

———————————————————

———————————————————

———————————————————

Amen

Jesus said, "Give, and it will be given to you; good measure, pressed down, shaken together, running over, they will pour into your lap. For by your standard of measure it will be measured to you in return."
Luke 6:38 NAS

"Bring all the tithes into the storehouse, that there may be food in My house, and try Me now in this," says the Lord of hosts, "If I will not open for you the windows of heaven and pour out for you such blessing that there will not be room enough to receive it."
Malachi 3:10

Prayers to Encourage and Comfort the Soul   125

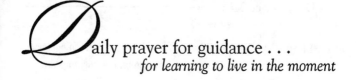

Daily prayer for guidance . . .
for learning to live in the moment

*I recommend having fun, because there is
nothing better for people to do in this world
than to eat, drink, and enjoy life. That way
they will experience some happiness along with
all the hard work God gives them.*

Ecclesiastes 8:15 NLT

Heavenly Father,

Life seems to be going by so quickly. I blink and my
children have graduated to another grade in school.
Barely a year passes and they've grown out of their shoes.
I stay so busy with motherly duties and responsibilities
that I rarely stop to enjoy the moment.

Lord, I want to savor these moments with my children. I
know they are Your gifts to me—fragile gifts that can
easily slip through my fingers. In the midst of my busy-
ness, give me a nudge, remind me to slow down and look
around, urge me to relish the simple joys available in that
moment of time. I thank You for each one.

Amen.

*I saw that there is nothing better for men than that they should be happy in
their work, for that is what they are here for, and no one can bring them
back to life to enjoy what will be in the future, so let them enjoy it now.*

Ecclesiastes 3:22 TLB

MY PERSONAL PRAYER

*God's gifts to mothers are often
delivered in small packages—gifts
of first hugs, fulfilled dreams,
healed hurts, life's lessons, and
simple everyday pleasures.*
Susan Duke

Dear Father:

_____

_____

_____

_____

_____

_____

Amen

*The earth and every good thing in it belongs to
the Lord and is yours to enjoy.*
1 Corinthians 10:26 TLB

*Jesus said, "So don't be anxious about tomorrow. God will
take care of your tomorrow too. Live one day at a time."*
Matthew 6:34 TLB

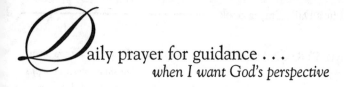

Daily prayer for guidance . . .
when I want God's perspective

You are my lamp, O Lord; The Lord shall
enlighten my darkness.

2 Samuel 22:29

Heavenly Father,

I'm just being honest—I can't see how anything good could possibly come from this situation we're going through. I'm just a simple human being. Without Your help, I'm stuck here, eyeball to eyeball with my problem.

Lord, I ask You to let me see things through Your eyes, just a glimpse, enough to give me a new perspective. How can I help my children see Your hand in this problem if I can't see it? Maybe there are things that You can't share with me, things I'm incapable of understanding, motives and considerations too high for my humanness. I accept that. I wait though, Lord, for You to show me what You can, a light at the end of the tunnel, hope in the midst of darkness. Open my eyes to see with new eyes.

Amen.

Fix your thoughts on what is true and good and right. Think about things
that are pure and lovely, and dwell on the fine, good things in others.
Think about all you can praise God for and be glad about.

Philippians 4:8 TLB

MY PERSONAL PRAYER

The higher your view of God, the higher your view of yourself.

Jan Carlberg

Dear Father:

_____

_____

_____

_____

_____

_____

_____

Amen

I will bring the blind by a way they did not know;
I will lead them in paths they have not known. I will make darkness
light before them, and crooked places straight. These things I will do
for them, and not forsake them.
Isaiah 42:16

God looks to the ends of the earth, and sees under the whole heavens.
Job 28:23-24

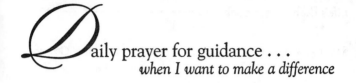

Daily prayer for guidance . . .
when I want to make a difference

*Jesus said, "Let your light so shine before
men, that they may see your good works and
glorify your Father in heaven.*

Matthew 5:16

Heavenly Father,

Thank You for my children. They are indeed my greatest
opportunity to affect the world around me, to make a
difference in time and eternity. I know that everything I
invest in them will be felt even after I'm a long time
gone from this earth.

If there are other ways that I could change the world for
Your holy purposes, I want to invest in those as well.
Open my eyes to see opportunities and give me the
insight to know what can be done, the part You intend
for me to play. I will be watching Lord, and I thank You
for what You have already entrusted to me.

Amen.

*You are a chosen generation, a royal priesthood, a holy nation, His own
special people, that you may proclaim the praises of Him who called you
out of darkness into His marvelous light.*

1 Peter 2:9

MY PERSONAL PRAYER

There is no power on earth that can neutralize the influence of a high, pure, simple, and useful life.
Booker T. Washington

Dear Father:

Thank you for the blessings of Baptism. Thank you for the fresh wind of the Holy Spirit in my soul. Help me to listen and obey. Help me to know you and trust you more that I might do Your Will.

Amen

Jesus said, "You are the light of the world. A city that is set on a hill cannot be hidden."
Matthew 5:14

It is the Lord's purpose that prevails.
Proverbs 19:21 NIV

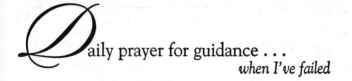

$\mathcal{D}$aily prayer for guidance ...
when I've failed

A righteous person may fall seven times and rise again.

Proverbs 24:16

Heavenly Father,

Forgive me for failing You. Forgive me and help me to forgive myself. I'm anxious to get this behind me. But before we move on, I ask that You would help me see clearly where I went wrong. Did I fail to listen to Your voice? Did I indulge in pride and selfish ambition? Whatever it was that brought us to this place, I want to see it for what it is so I won't make the same mistakes again.

I know, Lord, that my failures affect those I love. They keep me from being the person, the mother that I need to be. Therefore, I must accept responsibility and reach out to You to show me the error of my ways. Help me to learn all I can and then to find the courage to move on.

Amen.

You, O Lord, are a shield for me, my glory and the One who lifts up my head.
Psalm 3:3

MY PERSONAL PRAYER

Failure is the condiment that gives
success its flavor.
Truman Capote

Dear Father:

_____

_____

_____

_____

_____

_____

_____

Amen

Trust in Him at all times, you people; pour out your heart
before Him; God is a refuge for us.
Psalm 62:8
Strengthen the weak hands, and make firm the feeble knees.
Say to those who are fearful-hearted, "Be strong, do not fear!
Behold, your God will come with vengeance, with the recom-
pense of God; He will come and save you."
Isaiah 35:3-4

Praising God is one of the highest and purest acts of religion.

In prayer we act like men; in praise we act like angels.

Thomas Watson

Daily Prayers for Praise . . .

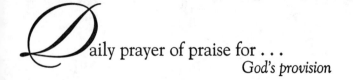

Daily prayer of praise for . . .
God's provision

*My God shall supply all your need according
to His riches in glory by Christ Jesus.*
Philippians 4:19

Heavenly Father,

I'm amazed by Your bountiful blessings. My heart
overflows with thankfulness for Your daily provision.
Even when situations look bleak and there are no
answers in sight, You come to my rescue. So many times
I've seen You put dinner on the table, when I could not.
I've seen You meet our needs when I could not.

I thank You for Your faithfulness. I know that my
children are safe in Your care. When I have done all I
can do, You are there for them. Your provision is
certain. It can be counted on. And for that I give You
all my thanks and praise. Receive it now from my heart
to Yours.

Amen.

*As you know him better, he will give you, through his great power,
everything you need for living a truly good life: he even shares his own
glory and his own goodness with us!*
2 Peter 1:3 TLB

MY PERSONAL PRAYER

Believe God's word and power more than you believe your own experiences. Your Rock is Christ, and it is not the Rock that ebbs and flows, it is your sea.

Samuel Rutherford

Dear Father:

_____

_____

_____

_____

_____

_____

Amen

Enter into His gates with thanksgiving, and into His courts with praise. Be thankful to Him, and bless His name. For the Lord is good; His mercy is everlasting, and His truth endures to all generations.
Psalm 100:4-5

Let us hold fast the confession of our hope without wavering, for He who promised is faithful.
Hebrews 10:23

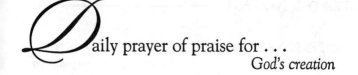

Daily prayer of praise for . . .
God's creation

The heavens are telling the glory of God; they
are a marvelous display of his craftsmanship.
Day and night they keep on telling about God.
Psalm 19:1-2 TLB

Heavenly Father,

The morning sunrise reminds me that once again You
have painted a canvas of beauty for my eyes to behold.
Your magenta brushstrokes across a buttermilk blue sky fill
my heart with wonder. I'm in awe of the twinkling stars
that hang like diamonds in the darkness above my head.

How do I find words for the praise that fills my heart
each time I hear a robin sing, or feel the softness of a
newborn kitten? You have surrounded me with beauty—
the beauty of Your creation. Thank You also, Lord, for
the beauty of Your human creation—for the sparkle in
my children's eyes and the uniqueness of their features.
I lift my praise to You.

Amen.

By Him all things were created that are in heaven and that are on earth,
visible and invisible, whether thrones or dominions or principalities or
powers. All things were created through Him and for Him.
Colossians 1:16

MY PERSONAL PRAYER

Earth's crammed with heaven, and every bush afire with God.
Elizabeth Barrett Browning

Dear Father:

_____

_____

_____

_____

_____

_____

Amen

The pastures are filled with flocks of sheep, and the valleys are carpeted with grain. All the world shouts with joy and sings.
Psalm 65:13 TLB

God made the beasts of the earth after their kind, and the cattle after their kind, and everything that creepeth upon the ground after its kind: and God saw that it was good.
Genesis 1:25 ASV

Prayers to Encourage and Comfort the Soul   139

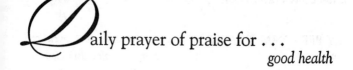

Daily prayer of praise for . . .
good health

> *Your light will break out like the dawn, and*
> *your recovery will speedily spring forth; and*
> *your righteousness will go before you.*
> Isaiah 58:8 NAS

Heavenly Father,

The first human bodies You created must have been quite amazing—full of healthy vigor and vitality. I know that was Your vision for all of us—until sin came into the world. Now, our bodies are always declining, breaking down with each new day.

I thank and praise You, Lord, for the way You often overrule illness and aging and bless us with good health. Your praise is on my lips as my child's fever subsides, as my strength is renewed each morning, as sickness is turned back at the door.

Even more, I praise You for the promise that one day we will receive new bodies—bodies like the very first ones You created, bodies that will never be ravaged by sickness or worn down with time.

Amen.

> *God said, "I will restore health to you."*
> Jeremiah 30:17 RSV

MY PERSONAL PRAYER

The body is the soul's house.
Shouldn't we therefore take
care of our house so that it doesn't
fall into ruin?
Philo of Alexandria

Dear Father:

_____

_____

_____

_____

_____

_____

Amen

Beloved, I pray that you may prosper in all things and be in
health, just as your soul prospers.
3 John 1:2

O Lord my God, I cried out to You, and You healed me.
Psalm 30:2

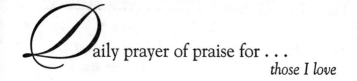

Daily prayer of praise for . . .
those I love

God is my witness, how greatly I long for you
all with the affection of Jesus Christ.

Philippians 1:8

Heavenly Father,

Thank You for my children, who remind me each day
that love is the greatest gift You have given us here on
earth. I praise You for every touch, every sweet kiss, and
every gentle embrace. I praise You for the bond of love
that ties me to them, that will not let me go, that fills
my heart with immeasurable joy.

I also thank You for the love You've poured out on
me—Your own child. Love that reached out to me
long before I could respond. Love that saw me not as
I was but as I could be. Love that found its way from
heaven to earth and gave itself for me. Love beyond
my understanding.

Amen.

Oh, how delightful you are; how pleasant, O love, for utter delight!
Song of Solomon 7:6 TLB

MY PERSONAL PRAYER

To love for the sake of being loved is human, but to love for the sake of loving is angelic.

Alphonse de Lamartine

Dear Father:

_____

_____

_____

_____

_____

_____

Amen

Love never fails.
1 Corinthians 13:8

You should be like one big happy family, full of sympathy toward each other, loving one another with tender hearts and humble minds.
1 Peter 3:8 TLB

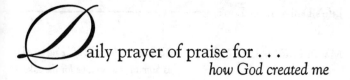

Daily prayer of praise for . . .
how God created me

> *I will praise You, for I am fearfully and wonderfully made; marvelous are Your works, and that my soul knows very well.*
>
> Psalm 139:14

Heavenly Father,

I praise You for the life You've given me. You formed me, You molded me, and You fashioned me in Your own image, a completely unique individual on which You have poured out Your love and caring. Thank You, Lord, for each talent, each gift. Thank You also for those things You've placed in me to motivate me to develop character and reach my full potential.

And, Lord, I thank You for making me a mother, for allowing me to partner with You in the miracle of birth. I take that seriously. Thank You for placing in me the capacity to love my children and raise them to be godly people. I will praise You before them all the days of my life.

Amen.

> *We are God's masterpiece. He has created us anew in Christ Jesus, so that we can do the good things he planned for us long ago.*
> Ephesians 2:10 NLT

MY PERSONAL PRAYER

*That which is striking and beautiful
is not always good; but that which
is good is always beautiful.*

Ninon de l'Enclos

Dear Father:

_____

_____

_____

_____

_____

_____

Amen

*You made all the delicate, inner parts of my body and knit
them together in my mother's womb.*
Psalm 139:13 TLB

*We are the clay and you are the Potter.
We are all formed by your hand.*
Isaiah 64:8 TLB

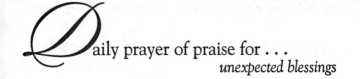

Daily prayer of praise for . . .
unexpected blessings

There shall be showers of blessing.
Ezekiel 34:26

Heavenly Father,

You are so gracious to me, sending this unexpected blessing my way. I enjoy giving unexpected gifts to my children, so I'm not sure why I would be surprised that You like to do the same. I just want You to know how grateful I am for this kindness.

Lord, I acknowledge that giving gifts is Your way. You are a giving God, who regularly pours out His blessings on His children. You are worthy of praise, Lord, and I give it freely, just as You have so freely given to me. I lift up my hands before You in thanksgiving and praise.

Amen.

You both precede and follow me and place your hand of blessing on my head. This is too glorious, too wonderful to believe!
Psalm 139:5-6 TLB

MY PERSONAL PRAYER

*God delights in surprising us. He
dots our pilgrimage from earth to
heaven with amazing serendipities.*
Charles Swindoll

Dear Father:

_____

_____

_____

_____

_____

_____

Amen

*The Lord's blessing is our greatest wealth.
All our work adds nothing to it!*
Proverbs 10:22 TLB

*You believed that God would do what he said; that is why he
has given you this wonderful blessing.*
Luke 1:45 TLB

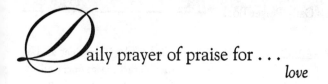

Daily prayer of praise for . . .
love

*My goal is that they will be encouraged and
knit together by strong ties of love. I want
them to have full confidence because they
have complete understanding of God's secret
plan, which is Christ himself.*

Colossians 2:2 NLT

Heavenly Father,

I've seen the power of love in my own life. I've seen it
transform a human life and light the flame of hope. I've
seen it reach out to the untouchables, and lift up the
fallen. I've seen it bring a smile to the face of a dying
man and give it's all for a stranger.

I set my heart to draw from that love every day. To pass
it along to my children and my loved ones. To give it
full and complete reign in my home. To let it fill me
and change me and make me more like You, Lord. Most
of all, I will praise You for it each day of my life.

Amen.

*We know how dearly God loves us, and we feel this warm love
everywhere within us because God has given us the Holy Spirit
to fill our hearts with his love.*

Romans 5:5 TLB

MY PERSONAL PRAYER

*Of all the earthly music, that which
reaches farther into heaven is the
beating of a truly loving heart.*
Henry Ward Beecher

Dear Father:

_____

_____

_____

_____

_____

_____

_____

Amen

*Walk in love, as Christ loved us and gave himself up for us,
a fragrant offering and sacrifice to God.*
Ephesians 5:2 RSV

All who love the Father love his children too.
1 John 5:1 TLB

Prayers to Encourage and Comfort the Soul   149

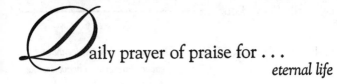

*D*aily prayer of praise for . . .
eternal life

> *Jesus said, "I give them eternal life, and they*
> *shall never perish; neither shall anyone snatch*
> *them out of My hand."*
>
> John 10:28

Heavenly Father,

I'll never forget the first time I heard the good news of Your love for me. On an old rugged cross, You died for my sins so that I might live forever. My heart leaps with thankfulness when I think of the eternal provision You gave me. As a mom, it's my responsibility to share this eternal gift with my children. Help me prepare them to receive You into their hearts.

One day, Lord, I will see You face to face, and I will be allowed to stay in Your presence forever. There I will be able to sing Your praises throughout eternity, unencumbered by the affairs of this life. I looking forward to that day—the day I will throw this life aside and begin to sing Your praises without interruption.

Amen.

God has given us eternal life, and this life is in His Son.
1 John 5:11

MY PERSONAL PRAYER

You shall sing His praise in a better place, a place that His hand has made.

Annie Johnson Flint

Dear Father:

_____

_____

_____

_____

_____

_____

Amen

Wait patiently for the eternal life that our Lord Jesus Christ in his mercy is going to give you.
Jude 1:21 TLB

Eternal life is in him, and this life gives light to all mankind.
John 1:4 TLB

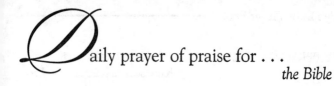

$\mathcal{D}$aily prayer of praise for . . .
the Bible

All Scripture is given by inspiration of God,
and is profitable for doctrine, for reproof, for
correction, for instruction in righteousness.

2 Timothy 3:16

Heavenly Father,

Your Word is powerful in my life. The more I read, the
more I praise You for giving me this beautiful and sacred
roadmap for living. From the beginning until the end of
the Bible, I find promises and encouragement through
the patriarchs who have lived before me. My heart is
enlightened with wisdom as I seek Your Word for all of
my needs.

I praise You for teaching me, correcting me, comforting,
and training me in righteousness through the Bible.
Thank You for all who faithfully transcribed Your
promises and truths for my benefit. Help me share the
treasures of Your Word with my children, giving them
an appreciation for the love letter You've written to us all.

Amen.

Whatever was written in former days was written for our instruction, that by
steadfastness and by the encouragement of the scriptures we might have hope.

Romans 15:4 RSV

MY PERSONAL PRAYER

The Bible is a telescope between
man and God; it is the
rending of a veil.
Augustus H. Strong

Dear Father:

_____

_____

_____

_____

_____

_____

Amen

Thy word is a lamp to my feet and a light to my path.
Psalm 119:105 RSV

Every word of God proves true.
Proverbs 30:5 NLT

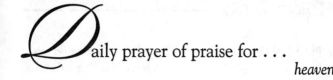

Daily prayer of praise for . . .

heaven

> *No eye has seen, no ear has heard, and no mind has imagined what God has prepared for those who love him.*
>
> 1 Corinthians 2:9 NLT

Heavenly Father,

I can only imagine what glory my eyes will behold when I finally see heaven. Your word describes it as a real place—a better country than earth. It's hard to comprehend walking on streets made of purest gold, touching gates bejeweled with precious stones, and dwelling in a kind of radiant light that shines without ceasing.

I praise You, Lord, that one day all pain and suffering will be erased, and there will be no more night. My heavenly home will take the place of what I often cling so tightly to on this earth. Your Word reveals that my true citizenship is in heaven, where the mansion you've prepared for me awaits. While I'm here, let me instill the vision of heaven in my children and share with them and others the glorious hope of our future.

Amen.

Jesus said, "In My Father's house are many mansions; if it were not so, I would have told you. I go to prepare a place for you."

John 14:2

MY PERSONAL PRAYER

Eternity is primary. Heaven must become our first and ultimate point of reference. We are built for it, redeemed for it, and on our way to it.

Joseph M. Stowell

Dear Father:

_____

_____

_____

_____

_____

_____

Amen

You are looking forward to the joys of heaven, and have been ever since the Gospel first was preached to you.
Colossians 1:5 TLB

Our citizenship is in heaven, from which we also eagerly wait for the Savior, the Lord Jesus Christ.
Philippians 3:20

Topical Index

You may pray for an hour and still not pray.
You may meet God for a moment and then
be in touch with Him all day.

Fredrik Wisloff

Additional copies of this book and other
titles from ELM HILL BOOKS are available from
your local bookstore.

Other titles in this series:

Life's Daily Prayer Book
Life's Daily Prayer Book for Teachers
Life's Daily Prayer Book for Women
Life's Daily Prayer Book for Graduates
Life's Daily Prayer Book for Fathers